The Queen Must Die

A comedy

David Farr

Samuel French — London
www.samuelfrench-london.co.uk

Copyright © 2003 by David Farr
Acting Edition © 2007 by David Farr
All Rights Reserved

THE QUEEN MUST DIE is fully protected under the copyright laws of the British Commonwealth, including Canada, the United States of America, and all other countries of the Copyright Union. All rights, including professional and amateur stage productions, recitation, lecturing, public reading, motion picture, radio broadcasting, television and the rights of translation into foreign languages are strictly reserved.

ISBN 978-0-573-05254-5

www.samuelfrench.co.uk

www.samuelfrench.com

FOR AMATEUR PRODUCTION ENQUIRIES

UNITED KINGDOM AND WORLD EXCLUDING NORTH AMERICA

plays@samuelfrench.co.uk

020 7255 4302/01

Each title is subject to availability from Samuel French, depending upon country of performance.

CAUTION: Professional and amateur producers are hereby warned that THE QUEEN MUST DIE is subject to a licensing fee. Publication of this play does not imply availability for performance. Both amateurs and professionals considering a production are strongly advised to apply to the appropriate agent before starting rehearsals, advertising, or booking a theatre. A licensing fee must be paid whether the title is presented for charity or gain and whether or not admission is charged.

The professional rights in this play are controlled by The Peters, Fraser and Dunlop Group Ltd, Drury House, 34-43 Russell Street, London WC2B 5HA.

No one shall make any changes in this title for the purpose of production. No part of this book may be reproduced, stored in a retrieval system, or transmitted in any form, by any means, now known or yet to be invented, including mechanical, electronic, photocopying, recording, videotaping, or otherwise, without the prior written permission of the publisher. No one shall upload this title, or part of this title, to any social media websites.

The right of David Farr to be identified as author of this work has been asserted by him in accordance with Section 77 of the Copyright, Designs and Patents Act 1988.

THE QUEEN MUST DIE

First presented at the Cottesloe Theatre as part of the National Theatre's Shell Connections Festival in July 2003.

CHARACTERS

The Girls
Shannon, fifteen
Lisa, fifteen
Sandra (also known as "Ronnie"), fifteen

The Boys
Darren Simpson, sixteen
Billy Simpson, twelve
Mad Mike, fifteen to eighteen
Shaun Digby, fifteen

Woman's Voice

SYNOPSIS OF SCENES

The action of the play takes place in a town in Middle England

SCENE 1 A wall in the rich part of town
SCENE 2 A wall on the poor side of town
SCENE 3 Margaret Chivers' living-room
SCENE 4 A wall on the poor side of town
SCENE 5 A wall in the rich part of town
SCENE 6 Margaret Chivers' living-room

Time — the night of 1st June 2002, the eve of the Queen's Golden Jubilee

THE QUEEN MUST DIE

Scene 1

A bit of wall somewhere in the rich part of a town in Middle England

The Lights come up. Three girls, all fifteen, are standing in front of the wall. They are Lisa and Sandra and Shannon. Lisa is small, mousy. Sandra is a little overweight, possibly. Shannon is the most glamorous of the three and carries a bag. All three are wearing simply horrendous home-made Union Jack dresses

Shannon We can't wear these.
Sandra I look like a flag.
Shannon I don't care if she's fifty years on the throne, or five hundred, we can't wear these.
Lisa Just think of it. Us dancing ——
Sandra — with a massive papier mâché statue of the Queen ——
Lisa — on a motorized float ——
Sandra — through the middle of town ——
Lisa — in front of the whole population.
Shannon I'll die.
Sandra You'll die! You're gorgeous and you still look like a dog. What must I look like?
Shannon Look at my tits, Lise.
Lisa What about them?
Shannon Is my point! I've got the best breasts in Year Ten. (*Searching the folds of the dress*) Where are they?
Lisa I've got tassles. Why did your mum give me tassles?
Shannon She said you were the tassles type.
Lisa I hate your mum.

Sandra Maybe we can blend into the background.
Lisa Ronnie, there is no background. It's us three, a papier mâché queen, and half a ton of bunting.
Sandra This is all your fault, Shannon Dobson.
Shannon Is not!
Sandra It was your idea to do a dance.
Shannon Was not!
Lisa Was.
Shannon Was not!
Sandra And then you roped us in because we weren't as good-looking as you.
Lisa Yeah, that's right, Shannon. If it wasn't for your vanity ...
Shannon I was told we would be dancing in glamorous gear to popular tunes of the five decades. I was told I could choose my costume.
Sandra I don't think your mum reckoned on a halter neck bikini.
Shannon That bikini was gorgeous.
Lisa You just wanted to show your arse off to Adam McEwan.
Shannon Christ, he's going to be there. This is worse than suicide.
Sandra He's going to get a right hard-on with you wearing that.
Shannon That does it. I'm not wearing this. We are not wearing this!
Sandra So what do we do?

Pause

Lisa Burn them!
Shannon Won't work.
Lisa Why not?
Shannon If we burn them, my mum will know it was us, and we'll be grounded for three weeks.
Lisa It's worth it, isn't it?
Shannon Three weeks Lisa.
Lisa So?
Shannon When is Britney at the NEC?
Lisa Two weeks tonight. (*Beat*) Oh.
Shannon Thank you very much.

Scene 1

Lisa We're screwed.

Sandra Hold on a minute. You only got two tickets for Britney and you've promised Lisa the other one. So what's stopping me burning mine?

Shannon One, because you're first reserve for the concert. And two, because if you burn your dress and make us do the Jubilee parade alone, we'll tell your mum about Mitchell Figgis and the bottle of cider.

Sandra You wouldn't do that. (*Knowing Shannon would*) You bitch.

Lisa So what do we do? Because I am not wearing this abomination in front of the whole town!

Shannon That's why I called the meeting. I've got a plan of action.

Lisa Go on.

Shannon First we go back to my mum and tell her how much we love the dresses.

Sandra That will be the biggest lie ever told by woman.

Shannon Second, free from all suspicion, we eliminate the queen.

Pause

Sandra Don't you think that's a bit extreme?

Shannon Not the Queen in Buckingham Palace. The queen that is currently sitting in Mrs Chivers' living-room in Penthall Gardens.

Lisa You mean...?

Shannon I mean if we can get in there without being noticed and destroy the statue, then there will be no queen, no float, no procession, and no ritual humiliation.

Sandra Wow.

Lisa But it's by an artist. He won a prize or something.

Shannon Who says?

Lisa It was in the paper. He's bringing art into the community. He's funded.

Shannon So what?

Lisa And he's staying with the Chivers' because they're great supporters of the liberal arts.

Shannon So what?

Lisa He made the queen in their garage. It's taken him four months.
Shannon I don't care if took him twenty years, I'm not wearing this dress.
Lisa And anyway the Chivers' will be there...
Shannon They're not there. Mr and Mrs Chivers are at a pre-Jubilee hoe-down in a barn four miles outside town. They've taken the artist with them.
Lisa The house is empty?
Shannon Not quite.
Sandra They've got a kid.
Shannon Which is being baby-sat.
Lisa By who?
Sandra By who?
Shannon By Shaun Digby.
Lisa Shaun "the lips" Digby?
Shannon "The lips" is all that stands between us and fashion safety.
Sandra How do we do it?
Shannon Lisa goes in, makes out like she fancies him and gets him upstairs. Then we sneak in and deface her majesty. When we're done, Lisa makes out like she had nothing to do with it, and he can't even say she was there, 'cos it would look like he was having girls in the house on the sly.

Pause

Sandra That is brilliant.
Lisa Excuse me. Why am I the one kissing Shaun Digby?
Shannon Everyone knows he fancies you.
Lisa He only fancies me because he knows he hasn't got a chance of getting you. He's just being realistic.
Sandra Don't be down about it, he's all right, is Shaun.
Lisa He's a minger! I'm not doing it.
Sandra I will.
Shannon He doesn't fancy you.
Sandra Oh.
Lisa I'm not doing it.
Sandra Go on, Lise.

Scene 2

Lisa No way.
Shannon Sandra, do you like Britney Spears?
Lisa That is blackmail.
Shannon She's playing the NEC, did you know that? I've got two tickets.
Lisa I'm not doing it, so don't even try it.
Shannon I think I've got the ticket here. (*She searches her bag*)
Lisa I'm growing out of Britney anyway.
Shannon (*finding the tickets*) Yeah, here we are.
Lisa Don't try it, girl!

Shannon slowly moves a ticket towards Sandra

Lisa All right, I'll do it! You're a bitch though. And I'm not kissing him.
Shannon You don't have to. Just use your charms.
Lisa He oils them lips, I swear he does.

Pause

Sandra So, while she's upstairs necking Digby — what exactly are we doing to the queen?

Black-out

Scene 2

A wall on the poor side of town

The Lights come up. Three boys are standing by the wall; they are Darren and Billy Simpson and Mad Mike Atkinson. Darren is sixteen, lean, dissatisfied with life, and very intense. Billy, his twelve-year-old younger brother, is in awe, and rather grubby. Mad Mike is Mad Mike — aged anywhere between fifteen and eighteen

Darren He said what?
Mad Mike He said he was busy.

Darren Busy doing what?
Mad Mike He didn't say, did he?
Darren Three months we've been thinking about this. Three months of precise planning. And now Les is busy. What would have happened to the French Revolution if the night before Danton had told Robespierre "Sorry, I'm busy".
Mad Mike I don't know. What would have happened?
Darren There would have been no French Revolution, that's what. France would be like England, ruled by a sovereign no-one has voted for, responsible to no-one, accountable to no-one, supported by centuries of privilege and living in five massive palaces for no reason that anyone can possibly understand. You know what? Les did this on the anti-globalization march as well. Remember what he said when he found out it was Starbucks we were protesting against?
Billy "But I like the fraps at Starbucks."
Darren "I like the fraps." That's not the point, is it? Try and get our useless generation to understand that politics requires commitment. It requires a level of sacrifice. We're talking about global slavery, extortion of the weak, we're talking basic human rights. So what if you can't get a frigging frappucino! Blow bubbles in your instant and stick it in the fridge!! Try to understand we're not little consumers in our little consumer worlds, we can't just pick and choose beliefs like we're in a sweet shop. Well, we'll show him. We'll do it on our own. Us three and Mary. That's all we need.
Billy Daz, about Mary.
Darren Now Mary understands passion.
Billy Daz.
Darren Mary is a flame, a beacon.
Billy About Mary.
Darren Where is she? I thought we agreed four-thirty. (*Pause*) What?
Billy Mary's not coming.
Darren What do you mean she's not coming?
Billy She left a message.
Darren Why didn't you say?
Billy I was gonna tell you but then you got all upset about Les.

Scene 2

Darren Why isn't she coming?
Billy She said ... She said it was because of last night.
Darren What about last night?
Billy You and her went out.
Darren What if we did?
Mad Mike Oh Christ, what happened?
Darren Nothing! We had a discussion about expressions of individual freedom in a post-romantic age, that's all.
Mad Mike Oh no.
Billy She said you got a bit intense, Daz. (*Pause*) I think you scared her a bit. Calling her Rosa Luxembourg and all that.

Pause

Darren She's not coming?
Billy She said maybe you should just leave things to cool for a while. She really likes you. But she's got GCSEs and everything. She hasn't got time for terrorism.

Pause

Darren OK. OK. Well, it's just us three. Or are you going anywhere, Mike? Am I too "intense" for you? Billy, check the alley.
Billy (*looking off*) All clear.
Darren Then I declare the meeting open. Firstly, as chair, I want to say something. The Popular Republican Front has been in existence for six months. Its stated aim: to offer protest against the imperialist and anti-democratic institution of the English Monarchy, in this the Jubilee Year. Our actions have so far been largely secret, involving discussion, and debate, and resulting in a series of resolutions as agreed at the last meeting. Billy, read the resolutions.
Billy (*producing a document and reading*) "One: that the monarchy is an anti-democratic institution existing only because of generations of privilege and injustice. Two: that the nation must be encouraged to debate the validity of said institution and to be

given the opportunity to vote on its continued existence. Three: that the impending Jubilee celebrations are an imposition on the freedom of every individual, funded as they are and as are all royal activities directly from the pockets of every British citizen. Four: that direct action of protest is a justifiable response. Five: that the said action may justifiably involve violence against capitalist property and symbols of establishment power but no violence against human kind is justified."

Mad Mike Or animal kind neither.

Darren Or animal kind neither. And now I ask you, Billy, as secretary, to countersign this statement which shall act as a manifesto for the group in the future.

Billy Where do I sign?

Darren (*pointing*) Just here.

Billy produces a pen and signs the document

OK.

Mad Mike So what are we gonna do? 'Cos my finger's getting itchy.

Pause

Darren Tomorrow a procession will make its way through the town. This procession will celebrate a tyranny that to this day keeps the British people in its vice-like grip. That makes us subjects where we should be citizens. That owns our executive, our lawmakers, that owns our church, our post, our theatres and opera houses. Even our government rules at her majesty's pleasure. And we sit like dogs lapping it up. Well, not any more.

Mad Mike What are we gonna do?

Darren We're going to stop tomorrow's procession.

Billy Are we going to chain ourselves to one of the floats, Daz?

Darren No Billy. That action, though ideologically sound, is practically flawed.

Mad Mike Pigs'll cut us out.

Darren Like they did at Newbury. No, our action must be something that we can say with absolute confidence will stop the

Scene 2

chariot of privilege in its corrupt tracks. Have either of you studied tomorrow's procession?
Mad Mike Tossers on floats, i'nt it?
Darren Six floats. The mayor has one, with some photographs of the town through the last fifty years. The Women's Institute have a small float celebrating the role of women in the Commonwealth. Mainly photographic material again, but they have a wreath of some kind. Following that are three of the primary schools, who are showing drawings and paintings that the children have contributed. Note how time and again the young are manipulated into collaborating with the established powers. And then ...
Billy Then what?
Darren Then there is the final float. A giant-sized statue of the Queen sculpted by an artist commissioned from taxpayers' money, will parade on a truck through the streets accompanied by young female dancers dressed in the Union Jack in a glorious and rousing tribute to Elizabeth Regina. *(Pause)* Or rather it won't.
Billy What do you mean, Daz?
Darren The queen will not be in a state to parade tomorrow morning. Because tonight, the Popular Republican Front will have conducted a ritual beheading of the sculpture, in the living-room of Margaret Chivers, a middle-aged arch-royalist who lives on the posh side of town.

Pause

Mad Mike We're gonna cut off her head?
Darren The execution will echo the beheading of Charles the First by the great revolutionary Oliver Cromwell. It will be filmed and we will deliver videos through significant letter boxes over the next few weeks.
Mad Mike Significant?
Darren Local press, local council, national press, the BBC, ten Downing Street, the House of Commons, the UN Council for Human Rights, and Nelson Mandela.
Billy Wow.

Mad Mike How we gonna do it?
Darren Leave that to me. Meet here at six tonight in dark clothing. Oh, one thing Mike. I'm counting on you for the axe.

Black-out

Scene 3

The living-room of Margaret Chivers' house

It is a well-kept and tidy room, with french windows leading into a garden and doors to the kitchen and to the hall; the house's front door is just visible through the hall door. A fireplace is set in one wall with a crockery-laden mantelpiece over it; more crockery is on display in glass cabinets. A three-piece suite dominates the room with a television facing it; next to the sofa is the giant statue of the Queen, covered by a cloth. There are other chairs and a telephone in the room. A birdcage with a canary in it hangs from the ceiling; the cage cover is nearby

The Lights come up. Shaun Digby sits on the sofa. He may be slightly overweight, and he may have unusual lips, or he licks them a lot. He is watching the television — a football match — and eating crisps.

There is an occasional chirp from the canary during the following

The phone rings. Shaun turns the TV sound off and answers

Shaun (*into the phone*) Hallo? Is that Mrs Chivers? ... How's the party? ... Everything's fine here. ... No, I haven't heard a peep from her. (*He looks at the queen*) I haven't heard a peep from her either. ... No, I'll make sure I don't spill anything on her. I know how important she is to you. Is the artist enjoying the hoe-down? ... That's good. ... About eleven? All right. (*He puts the phone down and sits*)

The phone rings again. He answers it

Scene 3

(*Into the phone*) Mrs Chivers? ...Yeah it's me. ... It's OK, Dad. You don't have to say that. ...I know you love me. I know you didn't mean it. ... Forget it, will you? ... Listen, the kid's crying, I better go. ... Love you too. (*He puts the phone down, returns to the sofa and sits. He eats some crisps*)

Lisa, nicely dressed up and carrying a bottle of alcopops, appears at the french windows and knocks on them

Shaun gets up and opens the french windows

Lisa All right?
Shaun Yeah.
Lisa Great.
Shaun What you doing in their garden?
Lisa I was just passing. Can I come in?
Shaun I'm baby-sitting.
Lisa I'll help you. (*She comes into the room*) Swanky place. (*She sees the covered-up queen; innocent as you like*) What's that?
Shaun It's the queen.
Lisa Oh, right.
Shaun It's for the procession tomorrow. The artist put a cover on it to protect it.
Lisa What's he like?
Shaun I think he may have a condition. He nodded a lot when I spoke to him.
Lisa I brought some alcopops.
Shaun What you doing here?
Lisa I was just on my way to Simon Miller's party, and I knew you were here so I thought I'd just pop in. Pop in to say hallo. (*A little alluringly*) You got a bottle opener?
Shaun I don't drink alcopops.
Lisa Nor me. But I thought seeing as it's just us we could try a few out. It's always worth trying something new, isn't it?

Lisa waltzes into the kitchen. She returns with a bottle opener, opening the bottle

Lisa You look really handsome in that top.
Shaun Do I?
Lisa You should wear that colour more often.
Shaun I always wear this colour.
Lisa Oh. Must be the light. It really suits you anyway. *Really* suits you. You want some?
Shaun All right.
Lisa What you watching?
Shaun The World Cup.
Lisa Oh, I love the World Cup. Who's playing?
Shaun I dunno. I don't watch it for the football. I just love South Koreans.
Lisa You what?
Shaun I'm going to emigrate to South Korea. I've sent off for the papers.
Lisa Why?
Shaun Because when they win a game they have this massive party in the streets and squares, a million people getting drunk and dancing and hugging each other, and then at midnight, someone blows a whistle, and they all pack up, tidy the litter up after them, and go home on excellent public transport. I think that's a kind of Utopia.

The phone rings

That'll be Mrs Chivers. She gets nervous being away.
Lisa From the kid.
Shaun From the statue. (*He picks up the phone*) Mrs Chivers? ... (*Quietly*) What is it now? You've already said that. ... Dad this really isn't the time. ... Of course I believe you. ... I swear I believe you. I've got to go, the kid's crying. ...Love you too. (*He puts the phone down*)
Lisa Is your dad not at the party?
Shaun He's at home.
Lisa With your mum?
Shaun No she's gone away for the weekend. She's not really a fan of the royals.

Scene 3

Lisa And him?
Shaun Oh, yeah. Yeah, he is.
Lisa Do you like my dress?
Shaun Yeah.
Lisa Do you really?
Shaun What you doing?
Lisa I've always really liked you, Shaun. I mean, I've always admired you. From afar.
Shaun Listen, maybe you'd be better off at the party.
Lisa I thought you liked me.
Shaun You know I do.
Lisa Well then, relax.
Shaun I just think you'd be better off at the party. If you want a good time, I mean.
Lisa I'm having a good time here.
Shaun It's just I'm not in a very "good time" kind of mood. No, honest, Lisa, I think you should go.
Lisa You haven't shown me round yet.
Shaun What do you want to see?
Lisa I don't know, I just fancy a quick tour. To the other rooms. Downtairs and — upstairs…
Shaun I'm not supposed to go into the rooms.
Lisa Live a little, Shaun.
Shaun I find living quite hard as a rule.
Lisa Come on, it'll be fun. No-one's going to catch us. (*Pause*) Listen. My dad said something to me once: you only ever regret what you didn't do.
Shaun OK. Wait there.
Lisa What you doing?
Shaun Shutting the windows.
Lisa No! Leave them. I might need to make a hasty exit if someone comes back. Don't want to take any risks, do we?
Shaun Lisa. If I ask you something, will you tell me the truth?
Lisa Of course, Shaun.
Shaun You're not taking me for a ride, are you?
Lisa What do you mean?

Shaun I just don't think I could cope if you were taking me for a ride.
Lisa Well, you'll have to find out, won't you?

They exit through the hall door

Immediately Shannon and Sandra appear through the french windows. Shannon has a pot of green paint

Sandra Give her credit. She didn't hold back.

They stop at the foot of the covered statue

It's enormous.
Shannon Get a chair.

Sandra moves away to pick up a chair; meanwhile Shannon pulls off the cover to reveal the statue. It is very life-like, if over-sized. Sandra returns

Sandra Oh, my God. It's her. It's really her.
Shannon Sshhh! Quick!
Sandra I mean it's really her. Our sovereign. I don't know if I can do this. I can't do it, Shaz. She'll be in my dreams.
Shannon Then hold the chair and I'll do it.

Sandra holds the chair and Shannon stands on it. Shannon opens the pot of paint and produces a brush

The doorbell rings. Pause

Sandra What do we do?
Shannon I don't know.
Sandra Do it quick and we'll run for it!
Shannon They'll see us.

Lisa enters from the hall

Scene 3

Lisa (*loudly*) I'll get it! (*Quietly*) Who is it?
Shannon I don't know. Where's "the lips"?
Lisa He's in the bedroom.
Sandra He likes you.
Lisa I'm gonna have to snog him in a minute, so you better get a move on.
Shannon Go back and say it was a Jehovah Witness. We'll text you when we're done.
Lisa Well, hurry up, I'm dicing with a greasy death up there!

Lisa exits through the hall door

Shannon (*to Sandra*) You answer it. Pretend to be the baby-sitter and get rid of them.

Shannon leaps down and hides behind the queen. Sandra opens the hall door, moves down the hall and opens the front door

Billy is revealed

Billy Hallo.
Sandra Hallo, I'm the baby-sitter. What do you want?
Billy I've lost my dog. Would you come and help me look for it?
Sandra Wait there. (*She closes the door on Billy and returns to Shannon*) It's just a kid. He wants me to help him look for his dog.
Shannon Go on. I'll paint her while you're gone.
Sandra See you back at base.

Shannon hides again. Sandra returns to the front door and opens it

Sandra (*to Billy*) All right then, but we must be quick, I have a baby to look after.
Billy Thanks.

Sandra and Billy exit and the front door closes

Shannon once again climbs on the chair and gets out her pot of paint. She prepares to smear green paint over the queen

Darren, with an axe, enters through the french windows into the room at a run

Darren is shocked to see Shannon and falls over the sofa; Shannon falls off the chair and ends up painting her own face

Darren Aaah!
Shannon Aaah!
Darren Who are you?
Shannon Don't kill me! I'll do what you say. Just don't kill me.
Darren I'm not going to kill you.
Shannon You look like you are.
Darren Who are you? What are you doing?
Shannon I was — just giving her some finishing touches.
Darren Who?
Shannon Her. I'm the artist's assistant. I mean I come from round here but I was given a placement — to assist. So I'm just — assisting ... Getting her really peachy for tomorrow.
Darren With green paint.
Shannon It's an art thing. You have to study to understand. What are you doing with that?

Pause

Darren I was chopping wood.
Shannon Oh right. Why?
Darren I was in the next door garden, when I saw you through the window and I didn't recognize you so I ...
Shannon Oh, you're a neighbour.
Darren That's right. We operate a vicious Neighbourhood Watch scheme and I was down the logpile when I saw this stranger with a paintbrush ...
Shannon Why were you chopping wood in June?
Darren I like to prepare for winter.

Mad Mike enters in Oliver Cromwell dress, with a video camera on a tripod. On seeing Shannon he falls flat to the ground

Scene 3

Mad Mike Who's she?
Darren It's all right, Mike, she's just the artist's assistant.
Mad Mike What's she doing here?
Shannon Who's he?
Darren Mike is — my brother. He was ... He was videoing me chopping wood. Weren't you, Mike?
Mad Mike I'm saying nothing!
Shannon Why's he dressed like that?
Darren Mike, why don't you go back home and I'll see you there?
Mad Mike I think we should kill her.
Darren No that won't be necessary.
Shannon He was filming you chopping wood.
Darren Yeah.
Shannon In that get-up.
Darren OK, the truth is we were doing a low-budget horror movie in the style of *The Blair Witch Project* in our back garden. And that's when we saw you through the window.
Shannon You make movies?
Darren Yeah. But I don't want everyone knowing.
Shannon I want to be in the movies. That's if I don't become an artist, of course.
Darren I reckon you could be in movies.
Shannon (*showing her good side*) Do you?
Darren Yeah. If you don't become an artist.
Shannon How many movies have you made?
Darren Quite a few.
Shannon Can I audition?
Darren Maybe not right now ...
Shannon But soon?
Darren Yeah, I reckon.
Shannon How will you find me?
Darren Which school you at?
Shannon Lee Bridge. You?
Darren St Peters.
Shannon That's in the shit bit of town isn't it?
Darren Yeah. So you've been working on the queen, have you?

Shannon Oh, yeah, yeah for ages. I really want her to look brilliant.
Darren You like the Queen, do you?
Shannon Don't you?
Darren Course we do. We think she's amazing. We think she's a true one-off. Don't we, Mike?
Shannon Yeah, I mean I would really hate it if anything were to happen to her tonight.
Darren Me too. I'd be furious. I'm a massive royalist. You are too, aren't you, Mike?
Shannon Give me more royal stuff, I can't get enough of it.
Darren I mean, if I had my way, they'd have more power than they do now. But there are some people who see it really differently...
Shannon Really? I don't know anything about that.
Darren Some people, for example, think it's weird that the Queen takes millions of taxpayers' money to live in massive houses that could be in the public domain, hoarding thousands of gardens, rooms, paintings and sculptures that should in reality belong to the British people.
Shannon That's just so blind of them, isn't it?
Darren I know. Some people think it's strange that the Queen still technically owns all the land of this country, including rivers, beaches — even the sea's hers. They think it's a bit odd that homeowners the country over don't actually own their houses at all, they're just owning it in her name.
Shannon I don't find that strange.
Darren Nor me. But there's no telling with some people. Personally, I just love the feeling of being a royal subject. And tomorrow will be the crowning moment of that.
Shannon You watching tomorrow, are you?
Darren Isn't everyone?
Shannon Yes, I suppose they are. Well, listen, I think I'm done really.
Darren You sure?
Shannon I was just touching her up. I'll be off now. I'm going. Maybe see you tomorrow, yeah?
Darren God save the Queen.
Shannon Yeah.

Scene 3

Shannon exits and closes the front door

Darren Collaborator!
Mad Mike We should have taken her out.
Darren And how would we do that?
Mad Mike She's seen our faces.
Darren Resolution number five. No violence against human kind is justified.
Mad Mike Or animal kind.
Darren Or animal kind.
Mad Mike You fancied her.
Darren I did not.
Mad Mike You fancy a royalist.
Darren Are we going to sit here chatting or are we going to set up the execution? Billy can't keep that girl looking for his dog all night.
Mad Mike Where do I go?
Darren On the chair.

Mad Mike produces a stocking and puts it over his head, then replaces his Cromwellian hat on top. He climbs on the chair with the axe. Darren places the camera in the middle of the room and lines it up on Mad Mike

Have you got the script I gave you?
Mad Mike (*producing the script*) Who wrote this shit?
Darren John Milton, the great republican poet and supporter of Cromwell.
Mad Mike Why can't he write plain English?
Darren It was plain in 1650. Get on the chair. Turn towards me. No, you're blocking the queen. Hold on. (*He covers the canary cage*)

The bird stops singing

Mad Mike What you doing?
Darren Stopping it singing.
Mad Mike That's cruel.
Darren It's only for a minute! OK, now do the whole arc of the swing without actually decapitating her, just for angles.

Mike does as ordered, stopping just before the neck

Darren And once more. Good. OK, I'm recording. Read it slowly and clearly and then perform the execution.

Mad Mike (*reading*) "It is lawfull, and hath been held so through all ages, for any, who hath the power, to call to account a tyrant, or wicked king, and after due conviction to depose and put him to death." (*He raises the axe to behead the sculpture*)

Darren Stop.

Mad Mike What is it?

Darren You should say "wicked king or queen".

Mad Mike It doesn't say that.

Darren But you should say it. Go again please.

Mad Mike "It is lawfull, and hath been held so through all ages, for any, who hath the power, to call to account a tyrant, or wicked king or queen, and after due conviction to depose and put him to death." (*He raises the axe*)

Darren "Him or her" to death. You should say "him or her".

Mad Mike I'll put you to death in a minute.

Darren OK, one more time. And this, time think about what the poor have suffered at the hands of this vixen, and mean it!

Mad Mike (*with sudden and great simple power*) "It is lawful, and hath been held so through all ages, for any, who hath the power, to call to account a tyrant, or wicked king or queen, and after due conviction to depose and put him or her to death!" (*He takes a huge swing, and is about to decapitate her majesty*)

Lisa enters

Lisa Will you get a move on, I'm virtually shagging the bastard. (*Seeing Mike*) Aaaah!!!

Mad Mike Aaah!

Mike swings, misses the queen and falls, embedding the axe in the sofa. A plume of duck feathers rises up around the room

Darren Who are you?

Scene 3

Lisa I'm ... I'm the baby sitter.
Darren You're what? You can't be. Who are you?
Lisa Who are you?
Mad Mike (*to Darren*) Don't say anything. Don't say anything! (*To Lisa*) Now you listen to me. You say nothing about this, you understand me? You came down, you tripped, and you split open the sofa. You never saw us, you never heard us. We do not exist. Is that clear? Or do you want an axe in your skull?
Lisa It's clear.
Mad Mike Let's go.
Darren What about ...?
Mad Mike I said let's go. (*To Lisa*) And remember. I know where you live!

Mad Mike and Darren gather their stuff, Mike just having time to lift the cloth off the canary cage. They exit

Lisa looks around for a second

Shaun (*off*) Lisa?
Lisa Oh no.

Lisa runs out of the french windows into the night

The stage is empty for a second

Shaun enters

Shaun Lisa, what are you ... ? (*He sees the mayhem. He sees Lisa is not there*) Lisa?

Silence. Shaun sits down and with a terrible quiet sadness puts his head in his hands. Then he starts to put the feathers back in the sofa

Black-out

Scene 4

The wall on the poor side of town

The Lights come up on Darren, Mad Mike back in ordinary clothes, and Billy. They have the Cromwell costume, camera and axe with them

Darren Why pull us out?
Mad Mike The operation was in danger.
Darren But we hadn't achieved anything!
Mad Mike We were at risk!
Darren She was just a girl!
Mad Mike I felt it was my responsibility, given the lack of rational leadership in the room, to order an immediate retreat.
Darren And now we haven't done anything! Yet again we've achieved nothing!
Billy Forty minutes I spent looking for a dog that doesn't exist. And all for nothing.
Darren (*to Mad Mike*) What did you say?
Mad Mike What about?
Darren Lack of rational leadership. Is that what you said?
Mad Mike What if it was?
Darren Are you saying I lacked leadership?
Mad Mike I'm saying you were too busy eyeing up that artist girl to pay attention to anything.
Billy What artist girl?
Darren That is not true.
Mad Mike This girl was in there, painting the queen when we arrived. You should have seen him. Giving her the eye. Telling her how much he loved the royals …
Darren That was cover!
Mad Mike He was so busy with the charm offensive, he forgot why we were there in the first place. So when the other girl came down ——
Billy Other girl?

Scene 4

Mad Mike — he was in no position…
Billy What other girl?
Mad Mike This other girl. Another baby-sitter. How do I know? The point is someone had to take control!
Darren I do not fancy her. She is a royalist, toe-sucking bitch!
Billy Three girls all looking after the house. That's a bit weird.

Pause

Darren Just what I was thinking.
Mad Mike What does it mean?
Darren They've been hired to protect the queen. Of course! Why didn't I think of it earlier. They must have suspected something like this might happen. Well, they're not beating us. Not this time. I am sick and tired of every one of our efforts coming to nothing.
Mad Mike Since when did my efforts come to nothing?
Darren Excuse me? Who organized the march against the nuclear power station? Who didn't check whether it was actually a nuclear power station and not a water cooling plant? Who tried to throw plant pots at Margaret Beckett and smashed the health food window shop? Useless! Pathetic! Well, not any more. We're going back, and boys, we are going to chop that royal head off if it kills each and every one of us. Who's with me?
Billy I'm with you Daz.
Darren Good boy Billy. Mike?

Pause

Mad Mike It was Claire Short.
Darren Mike.
Mad Mike It was Claire Short and she ducked! (*Pause*) I'm with you.
Darren OK. OK! Let's do it. Up the Republic!
All Up the Republic!

Black-out

Scene 5

The wall in the rich part of town

The Lights come up on Sandra, Shannon and Lisa

Sandra What happened?
Shannon I was interrupted!
Sandra Forty minutes I spent looking for that dog. We didn't even find it. The kid was distraught. He had tears rolling down his face.
Lisa I come down, she's not even in the room. This bloke's standing on a chair with an axe and the other one's filming him.
Sandra You what?
Shannon They're making this movie.
Sandra What are they doing making it in Mrs Chivers' living room?
Shannon They saw me while they were making the film next door. That's why I had to get out.
Sandra You were caught? We're going to get done.
Shannon We're not going to get done.
Sandra We could go down for that. Entering and Trespass.
Shannon Will you chill out? I told him I was the artist's assistant. He completely fell for it.
Sandra (*to Lisa*) What were you doing all this while?
Lisa I was keeping Shaun busy.
Shannon (*to herself*) I reckon he's a really good film director.
Sandra (*to Lisa*) Were you now? Did you kiss him?
Shannon (*to herself*) He might be the new Spielberg ——
Lisa I had to!
Sandra What was it like?
Lisa It was ...
Shannon — and I could be like Laura Dern in Jurassic Park. (*She mimes being afraid of a dinosaur*)
Lisa It was — really — really ... It was — I mean it was horrible, obviously ...
Sandra You loved it.

Scene 5

Lisa Did not!
Sandra You fancy Shaun Digby.
Lisa I do not!
Sandra How long d'you kiss him for?
Lisa I'm not the one fancying anyone. Listen to her waxing lyrical about Alfred Hitchcock. Doing a bloody screen test when she should have been getting the job done!
Shannon I was not waxing anything!
Lisa I would never have kissed Shaun if you hadn't taken so bloody long.
Shannon He came in as I was about to paint her green. What was I supposed to do? Just carry on smearing her majesty in Dulux gloss?
Lisa So what now?
Shannon We go back.
Sandra What if they're still there?
Shannon They won't be, they've got a filming schedule to keep to. Lisa can take Shaun upstairs for a bit more hot action —
Sandra — seeing as she enjoyed it so much —
Lisa Did not ...
Shannon — and this time we'll get it done. What do you say?
Sandra I'll give it one more go.
Shannon Prepared to snog Shaun for another twenty minutes or so?

Beat

Lisa All right.
Sandra That was hard.
Lisa I'm doing this for you, slag!
Sandra Sure you are, Lise. Sure you are.
Shannon And if the film director is still there, I'll deal with him.

Pause

Sandra I give up with you two, I really do.

Black-out

Scene 6

The living-room of Margaret Chivers' house

The Lights come up. The room is as it was at the end of Scene 3. Shaun Digby is carefully replacing individual feathers into the sofa

The canary sings occasionally during the following

The phone rings. Shaun answers it

Shaun (*into the phone*) Hallo? (*Beat*) Is that you, Dad? ... Dad, you're drunk. Stop shouting at me. ... Dad, I'm not coming home if you're gonna be like that. ... I don't know where I'll go. ... Dad stop it. I said stop it! Shut it! Shut it will you! (*He slams the phone down*)

The telephone rings instantly. He picks it up

(*Into the phone*) I said shut it, you pisshead! ... Oh, hallo, Mrs Chivers. ... No, everything's fine. I just had a hoax caller, that's all. ... Everything's great here. ... She's fine. ... She's fine, too. How's the hoe-down? ... Strip the willow? Cool. ... OK then, bye now. (*He puts the phone down and continues his feather-packing. He stops to swig more of the alcopops that Lisa left. I believe it's known as drowning one's sorrows*)

The doorbell rings. Shaun sighs. The bell rings again. Shaun moves to the front door and opens it

Darren, Billy and Mad Mike enter in stocking masks, with the axe, pushing Shaun back into the room

Darren Get down on the floor!
Mad Mike Down! Down! Down!
Darren Get down and you won't be hurt.

Scene 6 27

Mad Mike Down! Down Down!
Darren Who are you?
Mad Mike Down! Down!
Darren Who are you?
Mad Mike Down! Down!
Darren (*to Mad Mike*) He is down! Will you shut up! (*To Shaun*) Who are you? Where are the others?
Shaun What others?
Mad Mike Don't fuck with us!
Shaun There are no others.
Darren Billy, check the house!

Billy exits

So, who are you?
Shaun I'm just the baby-sitter.
Darren Don't mess me around!
Shaun I am! Honest!
Darren I've already met two other babysitters here tonight! Which organization do you belong to? You're trying to stop us, is that right?
Shaun I don't know what you're talking about!
Mad Mike I say we kill him.
Darren Shut it! (*To Shaun*) There were three girls in this house earlier, and no sign of you. So don't fuck with me, OK?
Shaun Three girls?
Darren One claimed to be the artist's assistant and the other two, babysitters. Now unless this is an exceptionally difficult toddler, I think three babysitters is a bit excessive don't you?

Billy enters

Billy All clear.
Darren Tie him up.

They tie Shaun up, and blindfold him

Darren You're just lucky you've fallen into the hands of an ethically responsible protest organization.
Mad Mike You royalist scum!
Darren Now sit there, keep quiet, and nothing will happen. Billy, get the chair.
Billy I've seen you before.
Darren Billy!
Billy Do you work in Asda on Saturdays?
Shaun Yeah. On dairy.
Billy That's it!
Darren Get the chair!

Billy fetches a chair

Darren rushes outside the front door, collects the camera, returns and sets it up

Mad Mike dons his Cromwellian uniform and axe and climbs on to the chair

Shaun What you doing?
Mad Mike None of your business.
Darren You don't know it, but you're witnessing history. You're witnessing the beginning of the end of one of the most oppressive regimes in the dismal record of man.
Shaun What do you mean?
Darren Just listen. You'll figure it out. OK, I'm recording. Read it slowly and clearly and then perform the execution.
Shaun What you doing?
Darren Will you calm down!
Shaun Don't kill me! Please, don't kill me.
Darren We're not executing you, you tosser.
Shaun Sounded like you were.
Mad Mike We will if you don't shut your mouth!

Darren covers the canary cage and the bird stops singing

Darren OK, I'm rolling.

Scene 6

Mad Mike (*producing the document and reading with terrific and dramatic conviction*) "It is lawfull, and hath been held so through all ages, for any, who hath the power, to call to account a tyrant, or wicked king or queen, and after due conviction to depose and put him or her to death." (*He raises the axe to behead the sculpture*)

The doorbell rings

Darren Cut!
Mad Mike Who is it now?
Darren How should I know?
Mad Mike (*to Shaun*) Who is it?
Shaun I don't know.
Mad Mike Talk!
Shaun I don't know, honest!
Mad Mike (*a cry of frustration*) Aaaah! We should have carried on with the execution!
Darren The doorbell was on the tape. You can't send that to Kofi Annan!
Mad Mike I don't give a shit about Kofi Annan! I just want to take that head off!

The doorbell rings again

Billy Get him to answer it. Like in a movie, he has to act dead normal and entice the person inside. Then we can deal with them too.
Darren Brilliant. (*He grabs Shaun*) Do it.
Mad Mike And listen to me. One false move, and you can forget resolution five, you'll be dead meat. Because I have had enough!

Shaun is untied and his blindfold removed. He goes to the front door. Darren and Mad Mike hide behind the living-room door. Billy hides behind the queen. Shaun opens the front door

Lisa is revealed

Lisa Hi.

Shaun Hi.
Lisa I'm sorry I disappeared earlier.
Shaun That's OK.
Lisa Can I come in?
Shaun Well ... Maybe now's not...
Lisa Don't be upset.
Shaun No, I really don't think now's the time...

But Lisa pushes Shaun into the living-room and starts to kiss him passionately. Billy, Darren and Mad Mike all come out from their hiding places. Lisa and Shaun kiss madly for a while more, then Lisa sees the three masked men

Lisa Oh my God.
Shaun That's kind of what I meant.

Billy and Mad Mike grab Shaun while Darren grabs Lisa and covers her mouth. The intruders blindfold Shaun and Lisa

Darren Don't move. You are in the hands of the Popular Republican Front. If you do not resist, no damage will come to you or your boyfriend.
Shaun (*extricating himself*) I'm not her boyfriend.
Mad Mike Shut it!
Darren Billy, let's get them upstairs and if you hear so much of a squeak out of them, kill them. (*He mimes to Billy "Not really"*) Get on the chair Mad Mike!

Billy and Darren march Shaun and Lisa, blindfolded and tied up, off

Mad Mike gets on the chair

Darren rushes in

Mad Mike Come on!

Scene 6

Darren OK, rolling. Go, go, go!
Mad Mike (*reading fast, with fury*) "It is lawfull, and hath been held so through all ages, for any, who hath the power, to call to account a tyrant, or wicked king or queen, and after due conviction to depose and put him or her to death!" (*He raises the axe to behead the sculpture*)

Shannon and Sandra burst through the front door, paint in hand, and run into the living-room

Shannon Let's do it!

Mad Mike falls off the chair and his axe goes through the mantelpiece, smashing a fair amount of crockery

What are you …?
Darren (*grabbing the axe*) Don't move! You are in the hands of the Popular Republican Front! If you try to resist us, we will kill the two hostages we have upstairs! Now sit down!
Shannon Is this in the movie?
Darren This is not a movie! This is very *very real!*

Billy enters

Billy What was the noise? Bloody hell.
Sandra That's the kid with the dog.
Darren Get upstairs and guard the hostages!
Billy They're don't need guarding. They're quite happy actually.
Shannon Aren't you film-makers?
Darren Do we look like film-makers? We're an action group, and if only you would stop interrupting us, we are here to behead this symbol of class corruption and societal decay that has held Britain in its icy grip for the last thousand years!
Shannon You want to destroy the statue?
Darren Yes, your beloved little statue, your little queen, whose face you were trying to make so perfect, I'm afraid that, come tomorrow, she won't have a face!

Shannon But that's what we want to do.
Darren What do you mean?
Shannon We're here to destroy the statue too.

Pause

Darren Don't even try it, "artist's assistant".
Sandra She's telling the truth.
Mad Mike I think we should kill them.
Shannon Why else would I have a pot of bright green paint? I was going to deface her but then you came in pretending to be neighbourhood vigilantes so I had to make something up.
Mad Mike Don't believe them.
Darren Shut it! (*To Shannon*) And the one upstairs?
Shannon She's part of it too! Her job was to get "the lips" out of the way. Go on, behead away, we won't stop you!
Darren Billy, go and untie the girl.
Mad Mike I say we kill them!
Darren And I am head of this organization! Billy go!

Billy exits

Sandra Where is she? What have you done with her?

Pause

Sandra You tied her up!
Darren We thought she was against us!
Sandra That's our mate, that is!
Darren How was I supposed to know? This is a major political operation, I had to make a quick decision! So what, you're not a royalist?
Shannon No way!
Darren And you really wanted to destroy the queen?
Shannon Yeah!

Pause

Scene 6

Darren I thought we were alone! I thought no-one felt as we did. It's unbelievable. Two groups, fighting for justice, for equality, for the end of privilege …
Sandra Well, not exactly …

Shannon kicks Sandra

Shannon (*to Darren*) Yeah, exactly.
Darren What's the name of your group?

Pause

Shannon Women Against the Monarchy. Or WAM for short.
Darren And you're the leader?
Shannon Of course.
Darren How long have you been preparing this?
Shannon Oh, ages.
Darren Months …
Shannon If not years. We've been completely focussed on it haven't we Ron?
Sandra Uh ... Yeah … Completely.
Shannon We're like totally underground. No-one's heard of us at all.
Darren But this is amazing. I thought we were alone. I thought no-one understood … No-one felt … No-one in the whole country … And all this time, on my own doorstep…
Shannon I believe in a world without class, a world without privilege, a world where men and women are free to live equally and in peace.

Sandra coughs

Darren A world without corruption.
Shannon A world without sleaze and scandal.
Darren A world of honesty, unstained by money, where men and women can live with each other

Shannon Love each other.
Darren And be at one with the beautiful world we've been given.

Pause. Darren and Shannon are close

Billy enters

I've untied her, but she doesn't want to come down.
Darren Billy, meet ——
Shannon Shannon.
Darren Shannon is the head of Women Against the Monarchy.
Billy What's your manifesto?
Shannon We think manifestos are old-fashioned. We believe in action and action alone.
Darren So do we.
Billy But what about the resolutions ...
Darren OK, listen. (*To Billy*) Shut it. (*To Shannon*) I have a proposal. I propose that the two movements unite in one action group, and that together we behead the queen as a statement of unified protest. Together we're stronger. What do you say?
Shannon Sounds good to me. I'd better ask my fellow sisters first though. Ronnie?
Sandra Whatever.
Darren Billy?
Billy I spent three days learning that manifesto.
Darren Billy!
Billy Together we're stronger!
Darren Good boy. Mad Mike?

Pause

Mad Mike What will the group be called?
Darren I don't know. People Against the Monarchy.
Mad Mike PAM.
Darren We can decide that later! I want to propose a joint execution of her majesty the queen by the Popular Republican Front and WAM.

Scene 6

Shannon Seconded.
Mad Mike How will the execution be joint?

Pause

Darren I want Shannon to do it.
Mad Mike She's not touching my axe.
Darren In the name of equality between groups ——
Mad Mike It's my axe!
Darren — you can stand next to her and read the words! But she has to do it! I film it. She does it! You read the words. Is that clear? Or do I have to question your allegiance?

Pause

Mad Mike (*handing Shannon the axe*) This is strictly a lend.
Darren OK, let's do it. Get on the chair, Shannon.
Shannon You're going to film me? I haven't put any make-up on.
Darren You'll have a stocking on your head.
Shannon Oh.
Mad Mike We're sending this to world governments. Do you want to be identified by the CIA, KGB and MI5?
Shannon Only asking.
Darren Have my stocking.
Shannon Thanks.

Darren takes the stocking off his head and gives it to Shannon. She puts it over her head and climbs the chair. She stands on the chair, very aware of her appearance

Darren Oh, that looks great.
Shannon You don't think I should get a shorter skirt?
Mad Mike Is this a fashion show or an execution?
Darren Rolling! Mad Mike, read it.

Pause

Mad Mike (*reading the document with grim determination*) "It is lawfull, and hath been held so through all ages, for any, who hath the power, to call to account a tyrant, or wicked king or queen, and after due conviction to depose and put him or her to death."

Shannon raises the axe to behead the sculpture. Lisa runs in

Lisa STOP!

Shannon swings, misses the queen, swings right round and knocks Mad Mike off the arm of the sofa. He smashes into a glass cabinet that falls on top of him. He lies still, his head bleeding heavily

Darren What are you doing?
Lisa You can't touch her! You mustn't!
Darren What are you talking about? Carry on with the execution!
Lisa I won't let you! (*She runs in front of the camera*)
Darren Get out of the way.
Shannon Get out of the way Lise, this is my great moment!
Darren Mike, pull the intruder out of the way!
Billy I think he's unconscious, Daz.
Darren Billy, pull her out of the way.
Lisa You have no idea what damage you will be causing if you go through with this!
Darren Are you a member of WAM or not?
Lisa What are you talking about?
Darren I thought you were supposed to be against the monarchy, not protecting it! What's going on here?
Lisa Shaun, come in!

Shaun enters nervously

Darren Who untied him?
Lisa I did.
Darren Are you insane? Why did you do that?
Lisa Because I love him.

Scene 6

Darren You what?
Lisa Shaun, tell them what you told me. About your dad.
Shaun I don't think I want to.
Lisa Tell them!
Shaun Lise ...
Lisa How many reasons does your dad have for being alive?
Shaun Three.
Lisa Name them.
Shaun Leicester City (*or other team*), the Queen, and beating the shit out of Mum and me.
Lisa What's happened to Leicester City (*or other team*) ?
Shaun They're relegated.
Lisa What's happened to your mum?
Shaun She's left him. Yesterday.
Lisa But she didn't take you with her.
Shaun No I think she forgot that bit.
Lisa So, if the Jubilee parade is cancelled, what will your dad have left?
Shaun Beating the shit out of me.
Lisa How much alcohol has he drunk so far this weekend?
Shaun Six bottles of beer, three bottles of wine and a quarter of whisky. That's when I left to come here.
Lisa How many more days off has he got for the Jubilee?
Shaun Three.
Lisa So you'll be alone with him for three days ... (*To the others*) That's why you can't touch her. If that parade goes ahead, Shaun's dad will be able to focus on the glory of Empire and Shaun will be spared. But if you execute her, you are condemning this boy to a living hell.

Pause

Darren Go ahead with the execution, Shannon.
Lisa You can't, Shaz...
Darren I'm sorry about Shaun and his dad, OK? But the fate of individuals cannot deter us from the wider aim.

Lisa What aim?

Darren The freeing of a whole country! Every liberating movement has caused suffering to individuals. You have to look at the greater good.

Billy What about resolution five?

Darren That's different.

Billy Why is it different? If he's gonna get leathered for the next three days because of us, how is that different ——?

Darren Because it's different! We won't hurt anyone ourselves. But we cannot legislate for every consequence of our actions ——

Billy That's not how I saw it.

Darren I don't care how you saw it! We're going ahead! We've been planning this for months, we're not stopping now for one sad bastard with a juiced-up father! We're action groups, not agony aunts!

Lisa Action groups?

Darren Before you came down it was agreed that the PRF and WAM should come together ——

Lisa What are you talking about?

Shannon Shut it, Lise!

Lisa What's WAM?

Darren What do you mean, "What's WAM?" You're in it.

Lisa What did she tell you?

Shannon Shut it or the queen's a goner.

Darren She told me about Women Against the Monarchy ...

Lisa What, that's us, is it?

Shannon I mean it, Lisa Edwards! If you want to spare your lover a beating ...

Darren What? What?

Pause

Lisa We're not members of Women Against the Monarchy.

Pause

Scene 6

Shannon You're dead.

Darren What do you mean?

Lisa We're not members of anything! We were going to do a dance on the motorized float with the statue and then we discovered we had to wear these really dog dresses and so we thought we'd come and deface her so the parade would be cancelled. That's the only reason we're here!

Shannon That is not true!

Lisa Is that true, Ron?

Pause

Sandra Yeah, that's true.

Shannon OK, maybe that's true for them, but I am a fully paid-up member of WAM. I'm politically motivated, I'm worthy of you and your group, and I will show you how much I believe in it now. (*She grabs the axe and the paper. Reading triumphantly*) "It is lawfull, and hath been held so through all ages, for any, who hath the power, to call to account a tyrant, or wicked king or queen, and after due conviction to depose and put him or her to death." (*She makes to swing the axe*)

Lisa holds up the Britney Spears tickets. Shannon stops her swing. Pause

Lisa Do it and I tear them up.

Shannon Where d'you get them from?

Lisa Nicked them from your wallet so you couldn't use them to blackmail me any more.

Darren What's going on?

Lisa Well, go on then. You give it to the queen, and I'll give it to Britney.

Shannon You won't do that, that's your ticket too.

Lisa Try me.

Shannon You worship her. You spend almost every day trying to be her.

Lisa I don't care.

Darren Britney?
Lisa Oh yeah, we're big on Britney ——
Darren But she's ... She's appalling ... She's the sickening epitome of US-led globalization, as perpetuated through the exploitation of young innocent children, turning still-growing kids into rabid consumers demanding ever more impossible levels of satisfaction.
Lisa — and we're seeing her in concert in two weeks time.
Darren (*to Shannon*) You cannot love Britney Spears and be who you say you are.
Shannon I don't love her. I think she's shit.
Darren Then what are you waiting for? Kill the queen.
Lisa Go on, Shaz. Kill the queen!
Darren Show me your beliefs, Shannon. The queen must die!
Lisa Do it, Shaz. Go on.
Darren Shannon, the queen must die!

Pause. Shannon slowly lowers the axe down by her side. Pause. Darren sits

How could you ... How could you say all that?
Shannon I'm sorry.
Darren Men and women — free to live in a world without class, without money ...
Shannon I'm sorry, OK. But Britney's just so cool. (*She remains standing on the chair with the axe by her side during the following*)

Billy approaches Darren

Billy It's all right, Daz, we'll find someone else to join us.
Darren No, we won't.
Billy Course we will.
Darren We won't! (*Beat*) I'm disbanding the group.
Billy You can't. We're still together! We're still strong!
Darren Strong? Look at us, Billy. Mary and Les have left. Mad Mike's unconscious. You're eleven and I'm just a sad loser. Face

Scene 6

it. No-one cares any more. Nothing's gonna change. Politics is dead.

Mad Mike suddenly stands

Mad Mike (*screaming; a cry of great vengeance*) Don't ever say that! Don't ever say that nothing's gonna change! (*He grabs the axe from Shannon and hurls himself at the queen*)

Shannon, Lisa and Sandra grab Mad Mike. There is a great fight. Mike makes one big swing and smashes the bird cage. There is a pause. Bird feathers fly everywhere

Look what you made me do! Look what you made me do! (*He drops the axe and collapses weeping on the sofa*)

A brief tableau. Cromwell lying on the sofa. Duck feathers. Canary feathers. Broken crockery. Broken glass. The queen, untouched, serene

Shaun goes over and looks at the queen

Lisa Is she all right?
Shaun Amazing. All around, destruction and chaos. And not a scratch on her.

The baby cries, off

There is the sound of a key in the front door lock. The door opens

Woman's Voice (*fruity; off*) We're back!

They all look at each other

Black-out

FURNITURE AND PROPERTY LIST

Scene 1

Personal: **Shannon**: bag containing Britney Spears tickets

Scene 2

Personal: **Billy**: document, pen

Scene 3

Set: Crockery on mantelpiece
Glass cabinets containing crockery
Three-piece suite; duck feathers in sofa padding
Cloth-covered giant statue of the Queen
Chairs
Telephone
Birdcage containing canary
Cage cover
Packet of crisps for **Shaun**

Off stage: Bottle of alcopops (**Lisa**)
Bottle opener (**Lisa**)
Pot of green paint, paint brush (**Shannon**)
Axe (**Darren**)
Video camera on tripod (**Mad Mike**)

Personal: **Mad Mike**: stocking mask

Scene 4

No additional properties

Scene 5

No additional properties

Furniture and Property List

Scene 6

Set: As end of Scene 3

Off stage: Ropes and blindfold (**Darren, Billy, Mad Mike**)

Personal: **Mad Mike**: blood sac

LIGHTING PLOT

Practical fittings required: television
One interior, 2 exteriors

SCENE 1

To open: General exterior lighting on wall

Cue 1	**Sandra**: " … are we doing to the queen?" *Black-out*	(Page 5)

SCENE 2

To open: General exterior lighting on wall

Cue 2	**Darren**: " … on you for the axe." *Black-out*	(Page 10)

SCENE 3

To open: General interior lighting with flicker effect from television

Cue 3	**Shaun** puts feathers back in the sofa *Black-out*	(Page 21)

SCENE 4

To open: General exterior lighting on wall

Cue 4	**All**: "Up the Republic!" *Black-out*	(Page 25)

Lighting Plot

Scene 5

To open: General exterior lighting on wall

Cue 5   **Sandra**: " ... I really do." (Page 25)
     Black-out

Scene 6

To open: General interior lighting with flicker effect from television

Cue 6   They all look at each other (Page 41)
     Black-out

EFFECTS PLOT

Cue 1	As Scene 3 begins
	Sounds of football match from TV;
	  occasional chirp from canary;
	  continue throughout scene
		(Page 10)

Cue 2	When ready *Phone rings*	(Page 10)
Cue 3	**Shaun** turns off the TV sound *Cut TV sound*	(Page 10)
Cue 4	**Shaun** puts the phone down and sits *Phone rings*	(Page 10)
Cue 5	**Shaun**: " … a kind of Utopia." *Phone rings*	(Page 12)
Cue 6	**Shannon** produces a paintbrush *Doorbell rings*	(Page 14)
Cue 7	**Darren** covers the canary cage *Cut birdsong*	(Page 19)
Cue 8	As Scene 6 begins *Occasional chirp from canary*	(Page 26)
Cue 9	When ready *Phone rings*	(Page 26)
Cue 10	**Shaun** slams the phone down *Phone rings*	(Page 26)

Effects Plot

Cue 11	**Shaun** swigs the alcopops *Doorbell rings*	(Page 26)
Cue 12	**Shaun** sighs *Doorbell rings*	(Page 26)
Cue 13	**Darren** covers the canary cage *Cut birdsong*	(Page 28)
Cue 14	**Mad Mike** raises the axe *Doorbell rings*	(Page 29)
Cue 15	**Mad Mike**: " … take that head off!" *Doorbell rings*	(Page 29)
Cue 16	**Shaun**: "And not a scratch on her." *Baby cries; sound of key in front door lock*	(Page 41)

www.ingramcontent.com/pod-product-compliance
Lightning Source LLC
Chambersburg PA
CBHW070636050426
42450CB00011B/3219